ECHO SHOW 5 (3RD GEN)

BEYOND THE BASIC

Discover Hidden Features, Transformative Upgrades, and Expert Tips for Maximum Enjoyment

JAMES SMITH T.

Table of Content

Chapter 1:...8
Getting Started With Echo Show 5 (3rd Gen)............ 8

Chapter 2:...20
Visual and Design Enhancements...........................20

Chapter 3:...31
Sound Quality Upgrades....................................31

Chapter 4:...43
Hidden Features You Didn't Know About................43

Chapter 5:...51
Game-Changing Upgrades.................................. 51

Chapter 6:...65
Pro Tips for Maximizing Your Echo Show 5.............65
Chapter 7:...84
Performance and Software Optimization................ 84

Chapter 8:...97
The Perfect Use Case for Your Echo Show 5...........97

Chapter 9:...110

Future Prospects and Updates..............................110

Chapter 10:..131

Troubleshooting and FAQ...................................131

CONCLUSION.. 137

INTRODUCTION

The Echo Show 5 (3rd Gen) is more than just a smart speaker; it's a revolution transforming how we interact with technology. From your bedside table to your desk, the sleek, compact design of this device hides an experience that's far more powerful than its size suggests. For years, the Echo Show 5 has been a popular choice for those seeking an affordable, functional smart display, but the third generation has elevated the game to new heights. If you've ever wondered if this small device could do more than just tell the time or play your favorite tunes, then you're in for a pleasant surprise.

The Echo Show 5 (3rd Gen) isn't just another smart display—it's a tool that can change how you live your day-to-day life. The second you unwrap it, you'll feel the difference. Imagine a clearer, more vibrant screen that's just as easy on the eyes in the middle of the night as it is in the daylight. The sound? Let's just say, it's no longer the afterthought it once was. With a revamped speaker system, it's ready to provide an experience that's rich, full, and immersive. It's easy to overlook the improvements when we've gotten used to certain expectations. But the Echo Show 5 (3rd Gen) isn't just about maintaining its legacy—it's about breaking barriers, providing an experience that surpasses what came before.

As you turn the pages of this guidebook, you'll uncover the Echo Show 5's hidden gems. You'll learn exactly how to navigate this upgraded marvel and squeeze every drop of value from it. This guide isn't just about the basics; it's a treasure chest filled with features you didn't know existed—game-changing upgrades that will transform how you interact with your Echo Show 5. Whether you're looking to amplify your sound experience, take control of your smart home in ways you never thought possible, or simply enjoy a smoother, more vibrant interface, this guide will ensure you get the most out of your device.

Step into the new era of Echo Show 5 with confidence. The 3rd Gen model is here, and it's time to see it for what it truly is—a powerful, versatile tool that can enrich your day-to-day life in ways you've never imagined. Let's dive in. The journey begins now.

Chapter 1:

Getting Started With Echo Show 5 (3rd Gen)

Opening the box of your brand-new Echo Show 5 (3rd Gen) is an experience in itself. As you pull back the packaging, you're greeted by the sleek design of the Echo Show 5, wrapped carefully to ensure no scratches or marks. It feels compact yet sturdy, with its soft fabric exterior and modern rounded corners. You'll notice the screen, protected by a thin layer of plastic film, hinting at the sharp, crisp display that awaits. Beneath the device, you'll find the power adapter and a quick-start guide to get you going. Now, let's dive into setting it up so you can get started right away.

1. **Remove the Echo Show 5 from its packaging:** Carefully unbox the device, along with the power adapter and quick-start guide.

2. **Connect the power adapter:** Plug the included power adapter into your Echo Show 5 and an electrical outlet. The device will power on immediately.

3. **Select your language:** Once the device powers up, the first prompt will ask you to choose your preferred language. Select the language you're most comfortable with.

4. **Connect to Wi-Fi:** The device will scan for available Wi-Fi networks. Select your network from the list and enter your Wi-Fi password to establish the connection.

5. **Log in to your Amazon account:** You'll be prompted to log in to your Amazon

account to link your Echo Show 5 with your Amazon services. Enter your credentials and proceed.

6. **Adjust basic settings:** Next, you'll set your time zone, adjust display preferences, and enable voice recognition to customize your experience.

7. **Connect your smart home devices (optional):** If you have smart home devices like lights or thermostats, you'll be prompted to link them to your Echo Show 5 for easy control.

8. **Personalize the device:** Customize settings such as screen brightness, volume, and other preferences to make the device feel tailored to your needs.

9. **Complete the setup:** Once the setup is complete, your Echo Show 5 is ready for use.

You can start exploring its many features, such as making video calls, asking Alexa questions, controlling smart home devices, and enjoying improved sound quality.

Step-by-step instructions for connecting your device to Wi-Fi and linking it with Alexa

Here are the step-by-step instructions for connecting your Echo Show 5 (3rd Gen) to Wi-Fi and linking it with Alexa:

1. **Power on your Echo Show 5:** After unboxing and connecting the power adapter to your Echo Show 5, plug it into an electrical outlet. The device will automatically power up and display the initial setup screen.

2. **Select your language:** When prompted, choose your preferred language by tapping on

the appropriate option. This will guide the setup process in the language you've selected.

3. **Connect to Wi-Fi:** The next screen will prompt you to connect to a Wi-Fi network. Your Echo Show 5 will scan for available networks nearby.

- **Step 1:** Tap on your Wi-Fi network name from the list of available options.

- **Step 2:** Enter your Wi-Fi password carefully, using the on-screen keyboard.

- **Step 3:** Once you've entered the correct password, tap "Connect" to establish a Wi-Fi connection.

    Note: Make sure your Wi-Fi connection is stable, and ensure your Echo Show 5 is within range of your Wi-Fi router for optimal performance.

4. **Sign in to your Amazon account:** After connecting to Wi-Fi, you will be prompted to sign in to your Amazon account to link your Echo Show 5 to your Amazon services.

- **Step 1:** Tap the "Sign In" button and enter your Amazon credentials (email and password).
- **Step 2:** Once logged in, the device will confirm your account and link it to your Echo Show 5.

5. **Enable Alexa Voice Recognition (optional):** Alexa uses voice recognition to personalize your experience. You can enable this feature by following the on-screen prompts.
- **Step 1:** When prompted, say the phrase "Alexa" so the device can learn your voice.
- **Step 2:** Alexa will confirm once it has recognized your voice, making your experience smoother when using voice commands.

6. **Test Alexa:** After your Echo Show 5 is connected to Wi-Fi and Alexa is set up, test the setup by asking Alexa a simple command like "Alexa, what's the weather today?" Alexa will

respond to confirm everything is set up and working properly.

7. **Complete the setup:** Once the Wi-Fi and Alexa setup are complete, you can move on to any additional customizations or smart device integrations. Alexa may suggest some smart home devices or Alexa skills to enhance your experience.

With these easy steps, your Echo Show 5 will be connected to Wi-Fi and linked to Alexa, ready for you to start using all the amazing features it has to offer!

How to navigate the touchscreen and buttons to get comfortable with your Echo Show 5

Here's a detailed guide to help you navigate the touchscreen and buttons on your Echo Show 5 (3rd Gen) for a seamless experience:

1. **Understand the physical buttons:** Familiarize yourself with the buttons on the top of the Echo Show 5.

   - **Volume Up (+):** Increases the speaker volume.

   - **Volume Down (-):** Decreases the speaker volume.

   - **Microphone/Camera On-Off Button:** Press this button to turn off the microphone and camera. When disabled, a red indicator light will appear to confirm the privacy mode is active.

2. **Explore the touchscreen interface:** The touchscreen is your main point of interaction with the Echo Show 5.

- **Swipe Down from the Top:** Opens the quick access menu, where you can adjust brightness, access settings, and enable features like "Do Not Disturb."
- **Swipe Left from the Right Edge:** Displays a series of customizable widgets, such as weather, news, or your calendar.
- **Tap Icons:** Select an app or feature by tapping its icon, just like on a smartphone or tablet.

3. **Interact with the home screen:** The home screen provides shortcuts to frequently used features.

- Look for rotating cards showing weather updates, calendar events, and Alexa suggestions.

- Tap any card to explore the information further.

4. **Adjust settings quickly:**
    - **Step 1:** Swipe down from the top of the screen to open the control panel.
    - **Step 2:** Tap "Settings" to access options for Wi-Fi, display, sound, and more.
    - **Step 3:** Use the back arrow in the top-left corner to return to the previous menu.

5. **Enable voice and touch integration:** You can use voice commands and the touchscreen simultaneously. For example:
    - Say, "Alexa, play music," and use the touchscreen to adjust the volume or skip tracks.

6. **Test gestures and actions:**

- **Swipe Left or Right:** Move between apps or screens.
- **Press and Hold on the Screen:** Open additional options for widgets or apps.

7. **Experiment with camera functionality:** If you use video calling or Drop-in features, ensure the camera toggle is on and adjust angles as needed for better visibility.

8. **Master basic commands:** Use voice commands to ask Alexa for help, or tap the on-screen Help icon to learn more about your device's features.

9. **Customize the interface:**
   - Go to Settings > Home Content to add or remove widgets and features displayed on the home screen.
   - Reorder your preferences to tailor the Echo Show 5 to your daily needs.

By practicing these steps and becoming familiar with the touchscreen and buttons, you'll feel confident navigating your Echo Show 5 and accessing its wide array of features.

Chapter 2:

Visual and Design Enhancements

The Echo Show 5 (3rd Gen) brings a fresh and refined aesthetic that elevates its functionality while adding a modern touch to your space. Let's dive into its standout design features:

1. **Infinity Glass Screen for an Immersive Display Experience:** The updated Echo Show 5 introduces an elegant glass-to-edge screen, creating a seamless visual flow. The display now feels more expansive, even though the screen size remains at 5.5 inches. This design not only enhances the aesthetics but also improves the clarity and vibrancy of the display. The screen's sharper resolution makes colors pop, whether you're viewing photos, watching videos, or reading content, delivering

an experience that's as visually appealing as it is practical.

2. **Rounded Corners for a Smoother, Modern Look:** Departing from the boxier designs of its predecessors, the Echo Show 5 (3rd Gen) embraces a smoother, more rounded shape. These subtle curves make the device feel less rigid and more organic, blending effortlessly into any room. Its compact design makes it ideal for bedside tables, desks, or countertops, adding a stylish yet unobtrusive touch to your décor.

3. **Enhanced Materials for a Sleek Finish:** Wrapped in a fabric exterior with matching buttons and a consistent color palette, the Echo Show 5 exudes sophistication. The all-fabric design eliminates the plastic edges seen in earlier models, resulting in a cohesive look that complements modern interiors. This improvement in build quality enhances both its

durability and tactile appeal, making the device a pleasure to use and display.

4. **Improved Nighttime Viewing:** This model's display optimization for nighttime use is a significant upgrade. The screen dims more effectively and displays content without the harsh glare often associated with screens in low-light environments. This thoughtful enhancement makes the Echo Show 5 an ideal companion for late-night use, whether checking the time, controlling smart home features, or enjoying calming visuals before bed.

5. **Compact Form with a Back-Firing Speaker Integration:** The redesigned shape also accommodates the upgraded back-firing speaker. This clever integration not only improves the sound projection but also streamlines the overall look, ensuring the device maintains its compact form without sacrificing audio quality.

6. **Attention to Detail in Button Placement:**
The top-mounted buttons align with the sleek design while maintaining easy accessibility. Their minimalistic appearance blends into the overall aesthetic, ensuring the Echo Show 5's functionality doesn't compromise its visual appeal.

These design enhancements reflect Amazon's commitment to combining practicality with style, making the Echo Show 5 (3rd Gen) a delightful addition to any environment. The thoughtful improvements ensure it not only performs but also looks great doing so, offering a product that appeals to both function and form.

How Amazon has optimized the screen for use in
low-light settings, improving readability and
comfort.

The Echo Show 5 (3rd Gen) introduces a thoughtful upgrade to its screen, making it more accommodating and user-friendly in low-light settings. This enhancement addresses a common challenge with devices that emit light in dim environments, ensuring the Echo Show 5 remains functional and comfortable no matter the time of day.

1. **Improved Nighttime Dimming for Subtle Illumination:** Amazon has fine-tuned the display's brightness to transition seamlessly between various lighting conditions. When the ambient light decreases, the screen automatically dims to a softer glow that is easy on the eyes. This feature is especially useful for bedrooms or other low-light spaces, as it

reduces the harsh glare that can disrupt your relaxation or sleep routine.

2. **Sharper Contrast and Clearer Text for Better Readability:** The screen's enhanced resolution and contrast adjustments ensure that text remains legible even in dim settings. Whether you're checking the time, reading a notification, or viewing a weather report, the improved clarity eliminates the need for squinting or adjusting your viewing angle, providing a smooth and stress-free experience.

3. **Adaptive Display Adjustments for Ambient Comfort:** The Echo Show 5 utilizes adaptive technology to calibrate the display based on the surrounding light levels. This means the screen not only dims but also adjusts its color temperature, offering warmer tones that reduce blue light emissions. This thoughtful addition makes prolonged use in low-light

settings more comfortable, helping to minimize eye strain during evening or nighttime hours.

4. **Enhanced Photo Frame Mode for a Cozy Ambiance:** When in photo frame mode, the screen maintains subtle lighting that doesn't overpower a dark room. Your selected images are presented with balanced brightness and natural colors, creating a warm and inviting atmosphere that enhances your living space without being disruptive.

5. **Seamless Integration with Nighttime Routines:** Paired with Alexa's nighttime features, such as alarms or sleep sounds, the optimized screen ensures your interactions remain discreet yet effective. Whether you need a quick glance at your schedule for the next day or want to adjust the room's lighting, the Echo Show 5 delivers an unobtrusive and intuitive experience.

With these advancements, the Echo Show 5 (3rd Gen) is perfectly suited for low-light settings, offering both comfort and utility. This makes it an exceptional choice for bedside use, evening routines, or any space where subdued lighting is preferred.

A side-by-side comparison of the new Echo Show 5's design against the older models.

The Echo Show 5 (3rd Gen) introduces several thoughtful design changes that elevate its appeal and functionality compared to its predecessors. By examining these updates side by side with older models, the improvements become clear, making it evident why the 3rd Gen is a significant step forward.

1. **Sleeker, Rounded Design:** The 3rd Gen Echo Show 5 replaces the more squared-off edges of its predecessors with a smoother,

rounded silhouette. This modernized aesthetic not only gives it a more refined appearance but also makes it easier to blend into various home settings. The compact profile has been slightly adjusted, resulting in a device that feels less bulky without compromising screen size.

2. **Infinity Glass-to-Edge Display:** One of the standout design upgrades is the glass-to-edge display. Unlike older models, where the screen was inset within noticeable bezels, the 3rd Gen offers a more seamless, edge-to-edge glass surface. This creates a more premium look while making the screen feel larger and more immersive, even though the physical dimensions remain the same.

3. **Improved Button Layout and Fabric Finish:** The button configuration on the 3rd Gen has been subtly refined, aligning it more closely with the Echo Dot (5th Gen). The buttons feel more tactile and intuitive,

enhancing usability. Additionally, the shift to an all-fabric design, replacing the previous models' plastic accents, gives the device a softer, more elegant finish that complements modern decor styles.

4. **Revised Speaker Placement:** The 3rd Gen introduces a rear-firing speaker design compared to the bottom-firing configuration of earlier versions. This change not only improves sound quality but also necessitates a slight adjustment to the overall shape, contributing to the rounded back. The result is a more cohesive design that prioritizes both aesthetics and performance.

5. **Camera and Connectivity Adjustments:** While the 2-megapixel camera remains unchanged, the back panel of the new model removes the micro-USB port found in older versions. This streamlining reflects Amazon's focus on simplifying the device and adding

functionality where it matters most, such as the optional stand with built-in USB charging.

6. **Enhanced Low-Light Screen Adjustments:** While older models featured basic brightness controls, the 3rd Gen excels with optimized low-light adjustments. The new display offers a better viewing experience in dim environments, making it ideal for bedrooms or nighttime use.

By refining the design elements that matter most, the Echo Show 5 (3rd Gen) not only looks more polished but also delivers functional enhancements that improve the user experience. These changes make it a compelling upgrade for both new users and those familiar with earlier models.

Chapter 3:

Sound Quality Upgrades

The new backfiring speaker design in the Echo Show 5 (3rd Gen) represents a significant advancement in sound performance, addressing many of the limitations found in previous models. By rethinking the direction and configuration of the audio output, Amazon has delivered a richer, clearer listening experience that enhances the device's overall functionality.

1. **Optimized Sound Direction:** Unlike the bottom-firing speaker design in earlier models, which caused sound to bounce off surfaces and dissipate unevenly, the 3rd Gen features a backfiring speaker. This change allows sound waves to project outward and fill the room more effectively. The result is audio that feels fuller and more immersive, even in compact spaces.

2. **Improved Bass Response:** The 3rd Gen boasts a significant improvement in bass performance. Despite the speaker only increasing slightly in size (from 1.65 inches to 1.7 inches), the new design leverages the top-back firing configuration to deliver twice the bass response of its predecessor. This adds depth and warmth to music and other audio content, making it more enjoyable to listen to at moderate volumes.

3. **Enhanced Clarity Across Frequencies:** The speaker's placement and firing direction contribute to better sound clarity, especially in the mid and high-frequency ranges. Vocals, dialogue, and instrumentals are now more distinct, ensuring a balanced audio profile. Whether you're streaming music, listening to news briefings, or making video calls, the enhanced clarity significantly elevates the experience.

4. **Performance in Various Environments:** The backfiring design also adapts well to different room setups. When placed in a corner or near a wall, sound reflections amplify the overall effect, creating a more dynamic listening environment. This flexibility ensures the device performs admirably, whether on a bedside table, kitchen counter, or office desk.

5. **Maintaining Sound Quality at Higher Volumes:** Previous models struggled to maintain audio quality at higher volume levels, often resulting in distortion. The 3rd Gen addresses this limitation by providing cleaner sound at volumes up to 70%, ensuring that even louder settings retain clarity and detail.

The backfiring speaker design is a thoughtfully engineered upgrade that transforms the Echo Show 5 (3rd Gen) into a more capable audio device. Whether you're using it to play your favorite playlists, set the mood with ambient sounds, or enhance video calls, the improved sound output ensures a versatile and enjoyable experience.

Analyzing the claim of "twice the bass" and testing the sound quality in real-world scenarios.

Amazon's claim of "twice the bass" for the Echo Show 5 (3rd Gen) is bold, but the real-world performance of this device provides tangible evidence to back it up. By addressing limitations in previous models and enhancing its audio capabilities, the 3rd Gen Echo Show 5 delivers a listening experience that feels significantly improved, especially in terms of depth and richness.

1. **Understanding "Twice the Bass":** The claim of doubled bass isn't just about volume—it's about creating a fuller, more

resonant low-frequency sound that adds depth to audio playback. Amazon achieved this improvement with a slight increase in the speaker size and a shift to a backfiring design. These changes allow the sound to expand more naturally into the room, creating a noticeable difference in bass response.

2. **Real-World Listening Tests:** In real-world scenarios, the enhanced bass is immediately apparent, especially when playing music genres like pop, hip-hop, or electronic, which rely heavily on bass lines. Comparisons with earlier models reveal that the 3rd Gen delivers a much warmer, more robust low end, while maintaining clarity in the mid and high frequencies. When tested with softer audio, like podcasts or classical music, the improvements are more subtle but still contribute to a richer overall sound.

3. **Performance in Various Spaces:** The 3rd Gen performs well in diverse environments, whether on a desk, a bedside table, or in a corner of the room. Placing the device near walls enhances the bass further, as the sound reflects and fills the space more effectively. This flexibility ensures that the claimed bass improvements aren't just theoretical—they're practical in daily use.

4. **Volume and Clarity Balance:** Maintaining sound quality at higher volumes has historically been a challenge for compact devices. In real-world tests, the Echo Show 5 (3rd Gen) delivers solid performance up to 70% volume, with minimal distortion. The bass remains tight, and the overall sound profile holds its integrity, making it suitable for casual listening in small to medium-sized spaces.

5. **Subjective User Experience:** While audio preferences are subjective, most users agree

that the bass improvement is both noticeable and enjoyable. The enhanced depth brings music and media to life in ways that earlier versions couldn't match. For users upgrading from older models, the difference is stark and immediately gratifying.

The "twice the bass" claim holds up well under real-world scrutiny. While it doesn't transform the Echo Show 5 (3rd Gen) into a dedicated audio powerhouse, it elevates the device's capabilities significantly within its category. For everyday use, the improved bass and overall sound quality make this model a standout choice, offering a richer and more immersive listening experience than its predecessors.

A detailed audio comparison to help you decide which device is best for listening to music and media.

When choosing a smart device for listening to music and media, sound quality is a crucial factor. The Echo Show 5 (3rd Gen) brings significant audio improvements, but how does it stack up against its predecessors and other Echo devices? Let's dive into a detailed comparison to help you determine the best option for your needs.

1. **Echo Show 5 (3rd Gen) vs. Echo Show 5 (2nd Gen):** The 3rd Gen model introduces a backfiring speaker design that transforms the listening experience. The 2nd Gen's sound output is hampered by its downward-firing speaker, which relies on surfaces to reflect sound. This leads to audio that feels muted and lacks clarity, especially in bass-heavy tracks.

In contrast, the 3rd Gen's backfiring speaker creates a more direct and expansive sound profile.

Bass is fuller, mids are more defined, and highs are crisper, making it better suited for both music and dialogue-heavy media like podcasts. If you're upgrading from the 2nd Gen, the improvement in sound quality is immediately noticeable.

2. **Echo Show 5 (3rd Gen) vs. Echo Dot (5th Gen):** The Echo Dot is known for its compact size and impressive sound for such a small device, but it doesn't feature a screen. When it comes to sound alone, the Echo Dot delivers comparable volume and clarity to the Echo Show 5 (3rd Gen), especially in the mid and high ranges. However, the Show 5 edges ahead with its richer bass response, thanks to the updated speaker design.

For users prioritizing sound and visual functionality, the Echo Show 5 (3rd Gen) offers an advantage. It combines improved audio performance with the added utility of a screen for displaying song lyrics, album art, or video playback.

3. **Echo Show 5 (3rd Gen) vs. Echo Pop:** The Echo Pop, with its more budget-friendly price, offers decent sound quality for casual listeners. However, it lacks the depth and clarity of the Echo Show 5 (3rd Gen). The Pop's sound is more one-dimensional, and its lack of bass presence makes it less suitable for music enthusiasts.

The 3rd Gen Show 5, with its balanced sound profile and improved bass, is a clear winner for those who value a fuller listening experience. Additionally, the Show 5's screen adds functionality that the Echo Pop cannot match.

4. **Performance Across Volume Levels**
Both the Echo Show 5 (3rd Gen) and Echo Dot (5th Gen) deliver consistent sound quality at moderate volumes. However, at higher volumes (above 70%), the 3rd Gen maintains its clarity and bass integrity better than the Dot and Pop. The 2nd Gen Show 5 struggles at higher volumes, with noticeable distortion and weaker bass.

5. **Suitability for Different Media:** For music, the 3rd Gen Show 5 excels in genres like pop, electronic, and hip-hop, where bass and clarity are essential. For podcasts or audiobooks, its balanced mids and highs ensure clear dialogue. While the 2nd Gen Show 5 and Echo Pop can handle casual listening, they fall short for more immersive experiences.

The addition of a screen makes the Echo Show 5 (3rd Gen) ideal for video playback and visual elements, adding versatility that the Dot and Pop cannot offer.

Final Recommendation

For users seeking an all-in-one device that delivers quality sound, visual functionality, and smart features, the Echo Show 5 (3rd Gen) is the best choice. Its audio improvements and additional screen utility make it a strong contender in its category. However, if you're on a tighter budget and prioritize sound over visuals, the Echo Dot (5th Gen) offers excellent value. For entry-level needs, the Echo Pop provides an affordable option, though it lacks the depth and versatility of the Show 5 (3rd Gen).

Chapter 4:

Hidden Features You Didn't Know About

The 2-megapixel camera on the Echo Show 5 (3rd Gen) might seem modest at first glance, but it's a versatile feature that significantly enhances video calls and home security. With practical functionality and thoughtful design, it caters to both communication and monitoring needs, making it an essential tool in your smart home setup.

The camera ensures clear video quality during calls, allowing you to connect with family, friends, or colleagues seamlessly. While it may not match the resolution of higher-end webcams or smartphones, the 2-megapixel sensor is well-suited for casual video chats. It balances sharpness and clarity, ensuring that you are visible without the need for excessive bandwidth, making it ideal for homes with varying internet speeds. Beyond communication, the camera doubles as a security feature. Through the Alexa app, you can access the live feed from your Echo Show 5, enabling you to check in on your home when you're away. Whether you want to monitor your pets, check if you've locked the door, or simply keep an eye on your living space, the camera offers peace of mind.

To optimize your experience, consider positioning your Echo Show 5 in a central location with a clear view of the room you want to monitor. Ensure it is placed at an appropriate angle for video calls, where the light source is in front of you to avoid shadows. For security use, avoid pointing the camera towards direct light or reflective surfaces, which could obscure the feed.

The camera also supports privacy-conscious users. A built-in shutter lets you physically block the lens when it's not in use, giving you full control over when and how the camera operates. For added security, you can disable the camera entirely through the device settings if needed.

Incorporating both video call and monitoring capabilities, the 2-megapixel camera on the Echo Show 5 (3rd Gen) provides a blend of convenience and practicality. By following these simple tips, you can maximize its potential, whether you're connecting with loved ones or ensuring the safety of your home.

A closer look at the stand's additional USB port for charging other devices while using your Echo Show 5.

The addition of a USB port on the new stand for the Echo Show 5 (3rd Gen) brings an extra layer of convenience to your smart home setup. This thoughtful design upgrade transforms the stand into more than just a way to adjust your device's angle—it becomes a versatile charging hub for your other gadgets.

The USB port on the stand allows you to charge compatible devices like smartphones, wireless earbuds, or fitness trackers directly from the same power source as your Echo Show 5. This eliminates the need for multiple outlets and reduces clutter, particularly in spaces like your bedside table, kitchen counter, or home office where extra charging ports are always welcome.

Using the stand is straightforward. Once your Echo Show 5 is mounted on it, simply connect your device's charging cable to the USB port located discreetly on the stand's base. The power is drawn directly from the Echo Show's adapter, so there's no need for an additional power supply.

The design of the stand is minimalist yet functional. Its clean lines and sturdy build ensure that your Echo Show remains stable while keeping the USB port accessible. This integration doesn't compromise the aesthetic appeal of your setup, blending seamlessly into any environment.

For optimal use, consider the charging needs of the devices you plan to connect. While the USB port provides convenient power, it may not deliver fast charging speeds for power-hungry gadgets like tablets. However, for smaller devices, it serves as a reliable and practical solution.

This small yet impactful feature exemplifies Amazon's commitment to making the Echo Show 5 (3rd Gen) a central part of your connected lifestyle. The added USB port not only enhances functionality but also helps you maintain a tidy, efficient, and tech-savvy space.

Exploring the new microphone setup that enhances voice command accuracy.

The Echo Show 5 (3rd Gen) introduces an upgraded microphone setup designed to improve the accuracy and responsiveness of voice commands. This enhancement ensures that Alexa can hear and process your requests more effectively, even in challenging environments.

The new microphone array is engineered to pick up your voice more clearly, even if you're speaking softly or from across the room. This is particularly useful in noisy settings, such as a bustling kitchen or a living room with background music or conversations. The improved sensitivity allows Alexa to respond more promptly, reducing the need to repeat commands.

To experience the full potential of this upgraded microphone system, position your Echo Show 5 in an open area, free from obstructions that might block sound. The design also accommodates scenarios where you might whisper a command—ideal for quiet moments, like adjusting the volume during nighttime or setting an early morning alarm without disturbing others.

When testing the responsiveness, users have reported that the 3rd Gen model consistently outperforms its predecessors in recognizing commands, even when multiple devices are connected in the same space. This reliability extends to various interactions, whether you're asking for the weather, controlling smart home devices, or initiating a video call.

Amazon's focus on refining the microphone system reflects their commitment to delivering a seamless smart home experience. With this enhancement, the Echo Show 5 (3rd Gen) not only becomes more intuitive to use but also sets a higher standard for voice-command technology in compact smart displays.

Chapter 5:

Game-Changing Upgrades

Here's a list of the key benefits of the AZ2 processor in the Echo Show 5 (3rd Gen), with explanations for each:

1. **Faster Load Times for Apps:** The AZ2 processor significantly speeds up how quickly apps open and load on the Echo Show 5. This means less waiting time for apps like music streaming services, weather updates, or video calls to start, giving you a seamless experience when switching between different tasks.

2. **Quicker Response to Alexa Commands:** Thanks to the enhanced processing speed of the AZ2 chip, your Echo Show 5 now responds more swiftly to voice commands. Whether you're asking Alexa for the weather, controlling smart home devices, or playing music, you'll

experience faster replies and actions, reducing any delay in responses.

3. **Improved Performance for Multitasking:** The AZ2 processor is designed to handle multiple tasks more efficiently. This means that even when you're multitasking—such as controlling lights while asking for news updates or making a video call—the device maintains smooth performance without noticeable lag or delays.

4. **Smoother Navigation Between Menus:** Navigating through menus, settings, and other options on the Echo Show 5 feels much faster. The processor allows quicker transitions and smoother scrolling, so moving from one feature to another feels more fluid and intuitive.

5. **Enhanced Video and Media Playback:** With the improved processing power of the AZ2, video calls, streaming services, and media

content playback are much smoother. Whether it's watching videos or making video calls, the device handles these tasks more efficiently, reducing stuttering and improving overall quality.

6. **Better Smart Home Control:** The AZ2 processor boosts the Echo Show 5's ability to manage multiple smart home devices at once. When you ask Alexa to control your lights, thermostat, or other connected devices, the Echo Show 5 handles these tasks more quickly, allowing for faster and more accurate home automation.

7. **Faster Software Updates:** The AZ2 processor also contributes to faster software updates and installations. This means that when Amazon releases new features or improvements, the update process will be more efficient, and your device will be able to take

advantage of the latest features with minimal disruption.

8. **Support for Advanced Features:** With the power of the AZ2 processor, the Echo Show 5 can better support advanced features, such as more complex voice interactions and enhanced image processing for camera-related tasks. This means that the device is capable of handling new features as they are introduced by Amazon, ensuring that your device remains up-to-date with the latest advancements.

By incorporating the AZ2 processor, the Echo Show 5 (3rd Gen) becomes significantly more responsive, capable of handling a wider range of tasks, and providing an overall smoother and more enjoyable user experience.

Echo Ship 1.1: A New Software Experience

Echo Ship 1.1 represents a significant shift in how the Echo Show 5 (3rd Gen) operates, providing a smoother, more intuitive software interface that enhances the user experience. Here's a breakdown of how this software update transforms the way you interact with your device:

1. **Sleeker, Faster Interface:** Echo Ship 1.1 brings a more streamlined and modern interface to the Echo Show 5. The menus and navigation have been redesigned for faster access and easier control. When you swipe through options or settings, everything feels more responsive, and actions happen more swiftly. The overall visual appearance is cleaner, with improved layout and faster load times for each function.

2. **Improved Visual Design:** The software now has a more polished and cohesive visual design, which complements the new hardware features

like the Infinity glass screen. Icons, text, and images are displayed with greater clarity and vibrancy, making it more pleasant to interact with the device. The visual update makes navigating your Echo Show 5's features more enjoyable, especially when using apps or viewing content like photos and videos.

3. **Enhanced Voice Control Experience:** With Echo Ship 1.1, Amazon has fine-tuned voice control capabilities to ensure that Alexa's responses are faster and more accurate. It is now easier than ever to issue commands for smart home controls, ask for information, or stream music, as the software has optimized the voice recognition process. Alexa is also quicker in processing and responding to requests, reducing any delays you may have experienced in the past.

4. **Fire TV-Like Interface:** One of the more noticeable improvements in Echo Ship 1.1 is the transition to a Fire TV-like interface when you

access multimedia options. Instead of a static display, it now includes a more dynamic and interactive layout that resembles what you might see on a Fire TV or other Amazon devices. This makes it easier to browse through media libraries, streaming apps, and settings.

5. **Smoother Multi-Tasking:** Echo Ship 1.1 also enhances the Echo Show 5's ability to juggle multiple tasks. Whether you're listening to music, checking your calendar, or controlling your smart home devices, the updated software handles these actions seamlessly. You can switch between different tasks with minimal lag, providing a more fluid experience when interacting with the device.

6. **Customization Options:** With Echo Ship 1.1, you have more control over customizing your Echo Show 5. The software update brings additional settings for personalizing the device's display, sound, and other preferences. Whether

it's adjusting your home screen layout or customizing the display for optimal viewing, you'll find that the software gives you more flexibility to make the Echo Show 5 fit your lifestyle.

7. **Consistent Updates and New Features:** Echo Ship 1.1 makes the Echo Show 5 (3rd Gen) future-proof by supporting consistent software updates. This ensures that you'll always have access to the latest features and improvements. Amazon can roll out new updates more easily, ensuring that the software evolves with new technologies and user needs over time.

In essence, Echo Ship 1.1 is a game-changer that significantly elevates the user experience, making the Echo Show 5 not just a smart display but a much more interactive, visually appealing, and intuitive device. With this software update, users can expect smoother navigation, enhanced voice control, and a better overall performance, all designed to enhance your daily interactions with the Echo Show 5.

The Fire TV-Like Interface: A Smooth Transition

The Fire TV-like interface introduced in the Echo Show 5 (3rd Gen) is a groundbreaking update that greatly enhances the way you interact with your device. If you've ever used a Fire TV or Fire TV Stick, you'll immediately notice the similarities. The goal behind this interface overhaul is to create a more dynamic, engaging, and user-friendly experience that ties together the device's functionality with a more polished and cohesive visual layout. Here's how this new interface changes the game:

1. **Dynamic Media Navigation:** One of the most significant changes brought by the Fire TV-like interface is how you navigate through

your media content. Instead of static menus and basic icons, you now experience a much more dynamic interface that displays content in a visually appealing way. Thumbnails of movies, shows, and other media appear as large, clickable images, making it easier and more intuitive to browse through different options. This brings the Echo Show 5 much closer to how you interact with a TV or streaming service.

2. **Improved Access to Streaming Apps:** With the Fire TV interface, your Echo Show 5 now offers quick access to a range of streaming services like Amazon Prime Video, Netflix, Hulu, and more. The layout mimics that of Fire TV devices, where you can seamlessly scroll through your subscriptions, recently watched content, and new releases. This streamlined access not only makes it faster to find something to watch or listen to but also ensures

that you're never far from your favorite shows or music.

3. **More Fluid User Interface:** Navigating through the Echo Show 5's settings, apps, and features has never been easier thanks to the Fire TV-inspired layout. The interface is now more fluid and responsive, with smoother transitions between menus and functions. Whether you're checking the weather, adjusting your smart home controls, or browsing through content, the new interface makes it feel like everything is just a few taps away. It's intuitive, simple to navigate, and offers a much more enjoyable experience than the previous, more basic layouts.

4. **Clearer Multimedia Experience:** The updated interface also enhances the way you view multimedia content. Whether you're looking at photos, watching a video, or checking out a weather forecast, the visuals are

presented more clearly and attractively. The screen itself pairs well with this upgraded interface, as the vibrant colors and improved display help make everything you see pop. It's an experience that feels more immersive and enjoyable, even when using the Echo Show 5 for everyday tasks like checking your calendar or viewing reminders.

5. **Customizable Layout for Personal Preferences:** One of the standout features of the Fire TV-like interface is its customization options. Users can adjust the layout to fit their preferences, whether that's changing how apps are displayed, reorganizing menus, or choosing what content appears first on the home screen. This flexibility means that you can create a home page that aligns with your unique needs and habits. Want to have your favorite news apps up front? Or perhaps prioritize your video streaming services? The new interface gives you the tools to personalize it all.

6. **Consistency Across Amazon Devices:** The Fire TV-like interface isn't just confined to the Echo Show 5 (3rd Gen). Amazon is slowly rolling out this design language across its entire lineup of Echo devices, from the Echo Show 8 to the larger Echo Show 15. This creates a seamless, consistent user experience across all of Amazon's smart displays, so if you're already familiar with Fire TV or other Echo devices, you'll feel right at home with the Echo Show 5. This consistency makes it easier to learn and use, no matter which Amazon device you have in your home.

7. **Streamlined Smart Home Control:** The Fire TV-like interface also enhances the way you control your smart home. The updated menus and options make it easier to interact with smart lights, security cameras, thermostats, and more. Everything is accessible from a single screen, and with just a few taps,

you can adjust settings or check the status of your devices. The layout is designed to make smart home control feel as easy and intuitive as possible, offering a simple yet powerful tool for managing your connected devices.

Overall, the Fire TV-like interface in the Echo Show 5 (3rd Gen) makes it an incredibly easy-to-use device, whether you're watching shows, listening to music, or controlling your smart home. The shift towards a more dynamic and visually appealing layout ensures that everything you do with your Echo Show 5 is both engaging and efficient. With this new interface, the device feels more like an integral part of your entertainment and daily routines, blending seamless navigation with advanced functionality.

Chapter 6:

Pro Tips for Maximizing Your Echo Show 5

One of the most powerful features of the Echo Show 5 (3rd Gen) is its ability to respond to voice commands through Alexa, Amazon's virtual assistant. As you get more familiar with your device, understanding how to use Alexa efficiently will elevate your experience. Whether you're controlling your smart home devices, accessing information, or simply having a conversation, Alexa is always ready to assist. Here's a guide to some essential voice commands that will help you master Alexa and unlock the full potential of your Echo Show 5.

1. **Basic Alexa Commands**
   - Start by getting comfortable with the foundational commands that make Alexa such a useful assistant. A simple

"Alexa" followed by a request will activate the device and get it listening. Here are some of the core commands to try:

- **Alexa, what's the weather today?:** This command will provide you with a detailed weather update, including temperature, precipitation, and other relevant weather conditions.

- **Alexa, set a timer for 10 minutes.:** Alexa will set a timer for the requested time and notify you when the time is up.

- **Alexa, add milk to my shopping list.:** This allows Alexa to keep track of your shopping needs, making it easier to organize and manage grocery lists.

- **Alexa, tell me a joke.:** A simple command that will prompt Alexa to tell a joke, great for lightening the mood or breaking the silence.

2. **Smart Home Control**

- One of the primary reasons people invest in Alexa-powered devices is for smart home control. The Echo Show 5 seamlessly integrates with various smart devices in your home. With just your voice, you can adjust settings, check the status, and even control appliances remotely. Try these commands:

- **Alexa, turn off the lights.:** If you have compatible smart bulbs connected to your Echo Show 5, this will turn them off instantly.

- **Alexa, set the thermostat to 72°F.:** Adjusting your smart thermostat becomes a breeze with this simple command.

- **Alexa, show the front door camera.:** If you have a smart camera connected, Alexa will pull up the live feed of your front door or any other camera you've set up.

- **Alexa, lock the door.:** This command works with compatible smart locks, giving you an easy way to ensure your home is secure.

3. **Media and Entertainment**

- The Echo Show 5 (3rd Gen) isn't just a smart speaker—it's a multimedia hub that can stream music, videos, and podcasts. Alexa makes it simple to enjoy entertainment on demand. Here are some commands to try:

  - **Alexa, play my workout playlist.:** Alexa will pull up your playlist from a connected music service like Amazon Music, Spotify, or Apple Music.

  - **Alexa, play [movie name] on Prime Video.:** With Prime Video linked to your device, you can watch movies and TV shows with a simple voice command.

- **Alexa, skip to the next song.:** Skip tracks in your playlist without needing to touch your device or app.

- **Alexa, stop the music.:** This command will pause or stop any media that is currently playing on your Echo Show 5.

4. **Managing Your Calendar and Reminders**
   - Alexa is an excellent assistant for organizing your day and keeping track of important events. You can use voice commands to set reminders, check your schedule, and plan your day effectively.

- **Alexa, add a meeting with John at 3 PM.:** This will add a calendar event to your schedule, keeping you on track for important appointments.

- **Alexa, remind me to take the medicine at 8 PM.:** Set a reminder for any task or event, ensuring you never forget important activities.

- **Alexa, what's on my calendar today?:** Alexa will read out your upcoming events for the day, giving you a quick overview of your schedule.

5. **Communication and Calls**
   - The Echo Show 5 (3rd Gen) is equipped with a 2-megapixel camera, making it a powerful tool for video

calling. Additionally, Alexa allows you to stay connected with loved ones through voice or video calls. Here are a few voice commands to help you communicate:

- **Alexa, video call Mom.:** Initiate a video call to a contact in your Alexa app, allowing you to stay in touch visually.

- **Alexa, drop in on [contact name].:** If you have enabled the Drop In feature, this command will connect you instantly with a friend or family member who has an Echo device.

- **Alexa, send a message to Sarah.:** You can also send text messages using Alexa, allowing you to stay in touch without needing to pick up your phone.

6. Exploring Skills and Features

- Alexa's skills are what make it an even more versatile assistant. Skills are essentially apps for Alexa, enabling it to perform a variety of functions. With thousands of skills available, you can ask Alexa to help with nearly anything. Here are some useful skill-based commands:

  - **Alexa, open the meditation skill.:** Use Alexa's skill to start a guided meditation session, perfect for relaxation or mindfulness.

  - **Alexa, tell me the news.:** Stay up-to-date with the latest news by activating one of the

many news skills available for
Alexa.

- **Alexa, play a trivia game.:**
  Engage with Alexa by playing
  games and quizzes, which
  provide entertainment and a
  fun challenge.

7. **Customizing Alexa's Responses and
   Settings**

   - A unique feature of Alexa is that you
     can personalize its responses to better
     suit your preferences. Whether you
     want Alexa to use a specific voice,
     change the language, or even make it
     funnier, these commands will help:

     - **Alexa, change your voice.:**
       Choose between different voice
       options to make your

interaction with Alexa more enjoyable.

- **Alexa, enable brief mode.:** Activate brief mode to shorten Alexa's responses, so she speaks less and provides quicker answers.

- **Alexa, change the language to Spanish.:** If you speak multiple languages, you can switch Alexa's language to any of the supported options.

Mastering these essential Alexa commands will unlock the true potential of your Echo Show 5 (3rd Gen). Whether you're using it for productivity, entertainment, or home automation, learning how to navigate Alexa's capabilities will make your experience smoother, faster, and more enjoyable. With regular practice, you'll find that Alexa becomes an invaluable tool that enhances every aspect of your daily life.

Using Echo Show 5 as a Digital Photo Frame

Using the Echo Show 5 (3rd Gen) as a digital photo frame is one of the most delightful features of the device. This functionality transforms your Echo Show into a personalized display, showcasing your favorite memories while blending seamlessly into your home decor. Here's how to get started and make the most of this feature:

1. **Link Your Photo Service:** Connect your Echo Show 5 to Amazon Photos or another supported photo service. Use the Alexa app on your smartphone to access the Photos section, where you can select albums or specific photos to display. This step ensures that your Echo Show 5 has access to the

images you want to showcase. For quick access, you can use voice commands like, "Alexa, show my vacation photos."

2. **Customize Slideshow Settings:** Adjust the slideshow duration, transition themes, and brightness settings to suit your preferences. This level of customization allows you to tailor the photo display to your mood or occasion. The vivid display on the Echo Show 5's edge-to-edge screen ensures your photos appear crisp and vibrant.

3. **Enable Ambient Lighting Adjustment:** The Echo Show 5 automatically optimizes photo visibility based on the surrounding light. Enabling the "Auto Dimming" feature lets the screen adapt to changes in room brightness, ensuring your photo frame doesn't appear too bright in dim settings or too dull in bright environments.

4. **Personalize Albums and Captions:** Organize your photos into themed albums, such as family events, vacations, or seasonal highlights. Adding captions can make your display even more engaging by providing context or special messages for each image. This personalization makes the Echo Show 5 feel more like a living photo album.

5. **Set Up Seasonal or Occasion-Based Rotations:** Create specific albums for holidays, birthdays, or other special occasions and enable them during relevant times of the year. This feature lets your photo frame reflect the current season or mood, enhancing its emotional connection.

6. **Integrate with Alexa Routines:** Enhance the photo frame functionality by incorporating it into Alexa routines. For example, when you say, "Alexa, start my morning routine," your Echo Show 5 can

display a specific photo album alongside the day's weather, calendar events, and news updates. This integration maximizes the device's functionality while keeping your memories in focus.

7. **Preview and Manage Photos with Voice Commands:** Use voice commands to preview or switch between albums seamlessly. Phrases like "Alexa, show my favorite photos" or "Alexa, play my family album" make navigating your photo collection effortless, especially when your hands are full.

By following these steps, your Echo Show 5 becomes more than a smart assistant—it transforms into a dynamic and customizable digital photo frame, ensuring your cherished memories are always on display.

Streaming and Watching Media on Echo Show 5

1. **Connect to Your Streaming Services:** To begin, link your favorite streaming accounts to your Echo Show 5 through the Alexa app. Compatible services include Netflix, Prime Video, Hulu, YouTube, and more. Navigate to the "Video & Music" section in the Alexa app, select your desired streaming platform, and sign in using your account credentials. This connection enables seamless access to your favorite shows, movies, and videos directly from the device.

2. **Using Voice Commands for Streaming:** Simplify media navigation by leveraging Alexa's voice commands. For example, say, "Alexa, play Stranger Things on Netflix," or "Alexa, open Prime Video." Alexa will automatically launch the specified app and begin playback. Voice commands

are particularly useful for quickly accessing content without needing to navigate menus manually.

3. **Customize Playback Settings:** Adjust your video preferences for an optimal viewing experience. Tap the screen during playback to access controls for brightness, sound, and playback speed. Use the device settings to enable closed captions or select preferred audio languages. The Echo Show 5's improved display ensures vivid visuals, even on its compact screen.

4. **Pair with External Speakers or Headphones:** For enhanced audio, pair your Echo Show 5 with Bluetooth speakers or headphones. Go to "Settings," select "Bluetooth Devices," and connect to your desired output device. This setup ensures an immersive experience for music videos, movies, or TV shows.

5. **Discover Live TV and News:** Use the Echo Show 5 to watch live TV and news updates. Alexa can integrate with apps like Hulu Live TV, YouTube TV, or specialized news platforms. Simply say, "Alexa, play CNN Live," to stay updated with current events. The compact design of the Echo Show 5 makes it a convenient media device for bedside tables or desks.

6. **Watch Short-Form Content on YouTube:** With built-in YouTube support, you can explore an endless variety of videos, tutorials, or entertainment clips. Use voice commands like "Alexa, play cooking videos on YouTube" to dive into specific genres or topics. The responsive touchscreen makes it easy to browse through recommendations and playlists.

7. **Optimize Viewing Angles with the Adjustable Stand:** If you're using the

optional Echo Show 5 stand, adjust the angle for a comfortable viewing experience. Whether you're cooking in the kitchen or relaxing on the couch, positioning the device correctly ensures clear visuals without strain.

By integrating robust streaming capabilities with an intuitive interface, the Echo Show 5 becomes an all-in-one entertainment hub. Whether you're binge-watching your favorite series or exploring new content, this compact yet powerful device delivers convenience and enjoyment in equal measure.

Chapter 7:

Performance and Software Optimization

1. **Enhanced Responsiveness for Daily Tasks:** The Echo Show 5 (3rd Gen) is powered by Amazon's AZ2 Neural Edge processor, designed to deliver faster performance across all its functions. Navigation through menus, opening apps, and executing commands feel noticeably quicker. Whether you're setting timers, checking the weather, or controlling smart home devices, the processor ensures a more seamless experience with reduced lag.

2. **Efficient Handling of Voice Commands:** The AZ2 processor significantly improves Alexa's ability to

process and respond to voice commands. This upgrade minimizes delays, especially for complex requests involving multiple actions, such as "Alexa, turn off the lights, play relaxing music, and set an alarm for 7 AM." The result is a smoother interaction with Alexa, allowing for faster execution of commands without repeated attempts.

3. **Optimized Local Processing:** Unlike older models that relied heavily on cloud-based computing, the AZ2 processor enables more tasks to be handled locally on the device. This shift reduces reliance on internet connectivity for routine actions, such as adjusting volume, controlling compatible smart home devices, or playing pre-downloaded playlists. By keeping these operations local, thEcho Show 5 offers a faster and more consistent performance, even in areas with weaker Wi-Fi connections.

4. **Improved Multitasking Capabilities:** The increased processing power also makes multitasking more efficient. You can seamlessly switch between checking your calendar, viewing photos, and streaming content without experiencing sluggishness. The ability to manage multiple apps or tasks simultaneously adds to the device's utility and enhances its appeal as a smart home assistant.

5. **Faster Smart Home Control:** When connected to a smart home ecosystem, the AZ2 processor shines by speeding up device discovery and control. For example, commands like "Alexa, turn on the living room lights" or "Alexa, lock the front door" are executed more quickly. The improved processor ensures real-time responses, making the Echo Show 5 an even more reliable hub for managing your home automation.

6. **Enhanced Video Playback and Streaming:** The processor contributes to smoother video streaming experiences by reducing buffering times and improving app launch speeds. Whether you're watching a tutorial on YouTube or streaming a movie on Netflix, the improved performance ensures that you spend more time enjoying content and less time waiting for it to load.

The inclusion of the AZ2 processor marks a significant leap in the Echo Show 5's performance capabilities. By delivering faster response times and greater efficiency, it transforms this device into a robust and dependable tool for both entertainment and productivity.

Addressing Cloud Slowness

1. **Understanding Cloud Reliance:** One of the key challenges with smart devices like

the Echo Show 5 (3rd Gen) is their dependency on cloud computing for many functions. Tasks such as fetching the weather forecast, syncing with external calendars, or retrieving information often involve sending data to the cloud and waiting for a response. While this design allows for advanced functionalities, it can introduce delays, particularly in areas with slower or inconsistent internet connections.

2. **Impact of Cloud Delays on User Experience:** Cloud reliance can sometimes lead to frustration, especially when a simple command like "What's the weather today?" takes longer than expected to respond. The delay disrupts the seamless experience that users expect from a smart device. These moments of slowness can be more noticeable when attempting to multitask, such as streaming media while controlling smart home devices simultaneously.

3. **Local Processing with the AZ2 Processor:** Amazon has taken significant steps to mitigate cloud-related delays in the Echo Show 5 (3rd Gen) by incorporating the AZ2 Neural Edge processor. This upgrade enables more tasks to be processed locally on the device, bypassing the need to communicate with the cloud for routine commands. For example, adjusting the brightness of the screen, controlling connected lights, or playing music from local sources are handled directly on the device, leading to faster execution times.

4. **Smart Home Automation Without Internet Interruptions:** With improved local processing, the Echo Show 5 enhances its role as a smart home hub. Actions like toggling smart plugs or controlling compatible thermostats are less affected by cloud latency. This improvement ensures

that your home automation remains responsive, even during temporary internet slowdowns.

5. **Minimizing Frustration with Predictive Updates:** The device's software also plays a role in reducing the perception of cloud delays. By predicting common user actions—such as opening frequently used apps or repeating routine commands—the Echo Show 5 can preload relevant data, reducing wait times for certain tasks. This proactive approach helps offset potential slowdowns when accessing the cloud for information.

6. **Suggestions for Overcoming Cloud Limitations:** For users looking to further minimize cloud-related slowness, keeping a strong and stable Wi-Fi connection is crucial. Positioning the device closer to your router or using a mesh network system can improve

connectivity. Additionally, regularly updating the device's software ensures it remains optimized for speed and functionality.

While cloud reliance is an inherent aspect of smart devices, the Echo Show 5 (3rd Gen) demonstrates how thoughtful hardware and software enhancements can significantly reduce the impact of cloud slowness. By balancing local processing with cloud-based capabilities, Amazon delivers a smoother and more responsive experience for users.

Troubleshooting Common Issues

1. **Connectivity Problems with Wi-Fi:** If your Echo Show 5 (3rd Gen) has trouble connecting to Wi-Fi, the first step is to ensure your network is working properly. Restart your router and modem, then try reconnecting the device. If the issue persists,

check that you're using the correct Wi-Fi password and that your network is compatible with 2.4GHz or 5GHz bands. You can also try moving the device closer to the router to strengthen the signal.

2. **Device Not Responding to Commands:** If your Echo Show 5 doesn't respond to your voice commands, ensure the microphone is turned on. A red light on the device indicates that the microphone is muted. Press the microphone button to enable it. Additionally, try speaking more clearly or closer to the device. If the issue continues, restart the Echo Show by unplugging it, waiting for 30 seconds, and plugging it back in.

3. **Screen Freezing or Lagging:** If the touchscreen becomes unresponsive or lags, perform a soft reset by holding the power button until the device restarts. Make sure your device is running the latest software

version by checking for updates in the settings menu. Clearing unnecessary apps or resetting the device to factory settings can also help resolve persistent performance issues.

4. **Audio Distortion or Low Sound Quality:** If you notice audio distortion or weak sound quality, ensure the speaker isn't obstructed or covered. Adjust the volume settings and test different sound levels. If the sound still doesn't improve, check for firmware updates that may enhance audio performance. Placing the device in a corner or near a reflective surface can also help amplify and balance the sound output.

5. **Camera Not Working for Video Calls:** If the camera doesn't function properly during video calls, confirm that it isn't physically covered. Check the camera settings to ensure it is enabled. If the issue

persists, restart the device and verify that the app you're using for video calls, such as Alexa's Drop-In feature, is correctly set up. Make sure the person you're calling also has a compatible device and an active internet connection.

6. **Alexa Skills Not Functioning:** If a particular Alexa skill isn't working, verify that it's enabled in the Alexa app. Disable and re-enable the skill to refresh its connection. Sometimes, restarting both the Echo Show and the Alexa app can resolve the issue. Check that the skill is compatible with the Echo Show 5 and updated to the latest version.

7. **Device Not Pairing with Bluetooth or Smart Home Devices:** For Bluetooth pairing issues, make sure the device you're trying to connect is discoverable. In the settings menu, select "Bluetooth Devices"

and try reconnecting. For smart home devices, ensure they are compatible with the Echo Show 5 and properly configured in the Alexa app. Resetting the smart device and reconnecting it often resolves these problems.

8. **Slow Performance When Opening Apps or Commands:** If you experience delays in app performance or command execution, clear the cache in the settings menu or restart the device. Disconnect unused accounts or apps that may be consuming resources. Ensure your internet connection is stable and that the device is updated with the latest software.

9. **Factory Reset to Resolve Persistent Issues:** If all else fails, performing a factory reset can help resolve persistent problems. Go to the settings menu, select "Device Options," and choose "Reset to Factory

Defaults." Keep in mind this will erase all personalized settings, so make sure to back up important data if necessary.

These troubleshooting steps cover the most common issues users may encounter with the Echo Show 5 (3rd Gen). With these solutions, you can quickly resolve problems and continue enjoying the full functionality of your device.

Chapter 8:

The Perfect Use Case for Your Echo Show 5

The Echo Show 5 (3rd Gen) is a powerful hub for managing your smart home, offering a seamless blend of voice control, touchscreen interactions, and Alexa-powered intelligence. Its ability to integrate with a vast array of smart home devices and simplify everyday tasks makes it an essential tool for creating a more connected and efficient living space.

Here are the step-by-step instructions for leveraging your Echo Show 5 for smart home control:

1. **Set Up Your Echo Show 5**
   - Connect your Echo Show 5 to Wi-Fi and link it to your Amazon account.

- Navigate to the settings and ensure Alexa is activated for smart home integration.

2. **Add Smart Home Devices**
   - Open the Alexa app on your smartphone or tablet.
   - Tap "Devices" at the bottom of the app and select "Add Device."
   - Choose the type of device (e.g., light, camera, thermostat) and follow the prompts to connect.

3. **Enable Smart Home Skills**
   - Search for specific smart home brand skills in the Alexa app.
   - Enable the skills and log in with your account credentials for each device's platform.
   - Sync your devices with Alexa for centralized control.

4. Customize Your Smart Home Dashboard

- On your Echo Show 5, swipe down from the top of the screen and tap "Smart Home."
- Arrange devices into groups (e.g., Living Room, Bedroom) for easier management.
- Pin frequently used devices to the home screen for quick access.

5. Set Up Alexa Routines

- In the Alexa app, go to "More" and select "Routines."
- Create routines by selecting triggers (e.g., "Good Night") and adding actions like turning off lights or locking doors.
- Test routines to ensure they perform as expected.

6. Control Devices with Voice Commands

- Use commands like "Alexa, turn off the lights," or "Alexa, set the thermostat to 72 degrees."
- For complex setups, use phrases tied to routines for automated actions.

7. **View and Control Devices on the Screen**
   - Swipe left on the Echo Show 5 to access the smart home dashboard.
   - Tap icons for real-time control, like adjusting light brightness or checking camera feeds.

8. **Monitor Your Home Remotely**
   - Enable Alexa Guard to monitor for sounds like breaking glass or alarms when you're away.
   - Use the Alexa app to check your devices remotely or view live camera feeds from your Echo Show.

9. Experiment with Advanced Features

- Explore third-party services for expanded functionality, such as IFTTT for custom automations.
- Integrate your Echo Show 5 with hubs like SmartThings or Zigbee for more robust smart home ecosystems.

By following these steps, you can unlock the full potential of your Echo Show 5 as the ultimate smart home command center, offering unparalleled convenience and control.

Using Echo Show 5 as a Bedside Clock or Desk Companion

The Echo Show 5 (3rd Gen) is perfectly designed to function as a versatile bedside clock or a practical desk companion. With its compact size, customizable features, and integrated Alexa capabilities, it fits seamlessly into any personal space, enhancing your daily routines and creating a more connected lifestyle.

Here are the steps to optimize your Echo Show 5 for use as a bedside clock or desk companion:

1. **Set Up Your Location and Time Zone**
   - Go to the settings on your Echo Show 5.
   - Select "Device Options" and set your correct location and time zone to ensure accurate time and weather updates.

2. **Customize the Clock Face**
   - Swipe down from the top of the screen and tap "Settings."
   - Navigate to "Home & Clock" and choose from a variety of clock face designs.
   - Personalize the clock with themes, colors, or even your favorite photos.

3. **Activate Night Mode**
   - Enable "Night Mode" under the "Display" settings to reduce screen brightness in low light.
   - Set a schedule for Night Mode to automatically adjust during your sleeping hours.

4. **Use the Alarm Feature**
   - Set alarms by saying, "Alexa, set an alarm for 7 AM," or configure multiple alarms for different needs.
   - Choose from a range of alarm tones or even use music or radio stations to wake up.

5. **Enable Do Not Disturb Mode**
   - Swipe down and tap "Do Not Disturb" to block notifications during specific hours.
   - Customize the schedule to ensure uninterrupted rest or focus time.

6. **Set Up Daily Reminders and Timers**

- Use Alexa to create reminders for tasks or appointments, such as "Alexa, remind me to take my medication at 8 PM."
- Utilize timers for activities like cooking or work sessions.

7. **Explore News and Weather Updates**

- Add news briefings or weather updates to your home screen for quick access.
- Say, "Alexa, what's the weather?" or "Alexa, play my Flash Briefing" to stay informed.

8. **Play Music, Podcasts, or Audiobooks**

- Connect your preferred music service, such as Spotify or Amazon Music, through the Alexa app.

- Use voice commands like "Alexa, play relaxing music" or "Alexa, resume my audiobook."

9. **Integrate Productivity Tools**
   - Link your calendar to the Echo Show 5 to view appointments and events.
   - Use the sticky note feature to jot down quick reminders or to-do lists on the home screen.

10. **Optimize as a Desk Companion**
   - Place the Echo Show 5 within arm's reach for hands-free video calls and quick Alexa commands.
   - Use the additional USB-C port on the stand to charge devices while working.

By following these steps, your Echo Show 5 can seamlessly adapt to your personal needs, whether as a soothing bedside companion or a productivity-enhancing tool on your desk. Its intuitive features and customizable options make it a valuable addition to any room.

<u>Understanding the unique benefits of Echo Show 5 in comparison to Echo Dot or Echo Pop.</u>

The Echo Show 5 (3rd Gen) stands apart from the Echo Dot and Echo Pop by offering a more dynamic user experience, thanks to its touchscreen display and enhanced functionality. Understanding these unique benefits helps highlight why the Echo Show 5 might be the better choice for specific needs.

1. **Touchscreen Display for Visual Interactivity:** Unlike the Echo Dot or Echo Pop, which rely solely on audio interactions, the Echo Show 5 features a 5.5-inch touchscreen. This display allows users to

visually access information, such as weather updates, calendar events, or recipe instructions, making it ideal for hands-on activities.

2. **Enhanced Entertainment Options:** The Echo Show 5 enables streaming from services like Prime Video, Netflix, or YouTube, offering a more immersive media experience compared to the audio-only playback of the Echo Dot or Echo Pop. Its screen also supports album art display and photo slideshows.

3. **Integrated Camera for Video Calls and Security:** The Echo Show 5's 2-megapixel camera facilitates video calls with loved ones through Alexa or Zoom. It also doubles as a security camera, providing a live feed viewable from the Alexa app, which neither the Echo Dot nor Echo Pop can offer.

4. **Visual Smart Home Control:** While all three devices support voice control for smart home devices, the Echo Show 5 provides a visual interface. Users can monitor cameras, control lights, or adjust thermostats with on-screen controls, making home automation more intuitive.

5. **Optimized Design for Personal Spaces:** The Echo Show 5's compact size, coupled with its multifunctionality, makes it an excellent bedside or desk companion. Features like Night Mode, a digital photo frame, and customizable clock faces add versatility and style to any space.

6. **Better Speaker Configuration for Media Playback:** The Echo Show 5 features a backfiring speaker design that delivers improved sound clarity and depth, including twice the bass of earlier models. While the Echo Dot offers decent audio, and

the Echo Pop focuses on compact sound, the Echo Show 5 strikes a balance with visual and audio enhancements.

7. **Multitasking Capabilities:** The Echo Show 5 enables simultaneous tasks like playing music while displaying lyrics, setting timers while showing countdowns, or using sticky notes for reminders. These multitasking features aren't as intuitive or available on the Echo Dot or Echo Pop.

By comparing these features, the Echo Show 5 proves to be a robust option for those seeking more than just a voice assistant. Its combination of a vibrant display, enhanced audio, and interactive capabilities makes it a standout device that bridges the gap between a traditional smart speaker and a multifunctional smart hub.

Chapter 9:

Future Prospects and Updates

As Echo devices evolve, it's exciting to consider the potential upgrades and features that could shape the future of smart home technology. Here's a look at what's next for Echo devices, based on current trends and innovations in the industry:

1. **Increased Integration with Smart Home Devices:** Echo devices are increasingly becoming the central hub for smart homes. Amazon will likely continue to expand their compatibility with a broader range of smart home products, from lighting and thermostats to security systems and appliances. Expect smoother integrations, better cross-platform compatibility, and perhaps even the ability to control more non-Amazon products seamlessly.

2. **Improved Voice and Sound Technology:** With each iteration of the Echo line, sound quality and voice recognition have improved. As Echo devices continue to improve, we can anticipate further advancements in audio, including better clarity, depth, and more sophisticated soundstage adjustments. Likewise, voice recognition will become even more accurate, particularly in noisy environments or when voices are mixed. Echo devices may also become more context-aware, offering smarter, more personalized responses based on the user's habits and preferences.

3. **AI-Powered Personalization:** Artificial Intelligence is already a key component in Echo devices, but future models could feature even more advanced AI, offering a higher degree of personalization. For example, Echo devices may recognize the

individual voices of everyone in the household and tailor responses based on their needs, preferences, or even mood. AI may also drive more predictive features, like automatically adjusting your home's temperature or lighting based on your schedule or habits.

4. **More Advanced Displays:** As seen with the Echo Show 5's improvements, Amazon is focusing on improving the visual aspect of its Echo devices. Future Echo Shows could feature higher-resolution displays, larger screens, or even foldable displays, allowing for more versatility in video calls, media streaming, and photo viewing. With better screens, Echo devices could serve even more purposes, from interactive learning tools to portable entertainment hubs.

5. **Enhanced Privacy and Security Features:** As privacy becomes an

increasingly significant concern, Amazon will likely enhance the security features of its Echo devices. This could include more granular privacy controls, such as improved muting options or smarter management of personal data. Expect Echo devices to continue to improve at detecting potential security threats, such as unauthorized access or potential vulnerabilities, and to offer more transparency around how data is used and stored.

6. **More Robust Integration with Health and Wellness:** Echo devices might continue to expand their role in health and wellness. Integration with fitness trackers, health apps, and even personalized health monitoring could make Echo devices more indispensable to users' daily routines. Imagine using Echo to track your sleep, monitor heart rate, or suggest personalized

wellness routines based on voice analysis or environmental data from within the home.

7. Advanced Multi-Device Functionality

Echo devices may evolve to work even more seamlessly as part of a multi-device system. Whether it's for streaming, gaming, or home automation, expect improved capabilities for linking multiple Echo devices together to create a more immersive or responsive experience. Features like synchronized sound, multi-room audio, or even multi-screen displays could become standard across the Echo ecosystem.

8. Sustainability Improvements: With growing concerns around sustainability, Amazon is likely to make future Echo devices more eco-friendly. This could mean using recycled materials in production, reducing energy consumption, and improving product longevity through software updates that ensure long-term usability without the need for frequent hardware upgrades.

9. Integration with Augmented Reality (AR) and Virtual Reality (VR):

As AR and VR technologies become more mainstream, Echo devices could evolve to integrate with these emerging fields. Imagine a future where Echo devices act as hubs for immersive experiences, helping users interact with virtual environments or overlay useful information on the physical world. A combination of AR glasses and Echo devices could open up entirely new dimensions for productivity, entertainment, and education.

10. Smarter Automation

Expect Echo devices to become more intuitive in automating everyday tasks. These devices will likely learn user patterns to better anticipate needs without explicit commands. From cooking to scheduling, shopping, and even sending reminders, Echo devices could take on more responsibilities in managing household tasks and personal productivity.

As Amazon continues to push the boundaries of voice assistants and smart home technology, Echo devices will undoubtedly grow more sophisticated. With each new release, Amazon's focus on user experience, convenience, and personalization will help drive the evolution of smart home ecosystems. Whether through smarter AI, enhanced privacy, or expanded functionality, the future of Echo devices promises to make them even more integral to daily life.

What kind of updates you can expect to further improve your Echo Show 5.

As technology continues to evolve, so too will the updates and improvements for your Echo Show 5. Amazon regularly rolls out software updates to enhance performance, introduce new features, and fix bugs. Here are some potential updates you can expect to further improve your Echo Show 5:

1. Enhanced Voice Recognition and AI Capabilities

One of the primary updates you'll see is improvements in voice recognition technology. Amazon is likely to continue refining Alexa's ability to recognize different voices more accurately, even in noisy environments. As Alexa becomes smarter, you'll experience more personalized responses tailored to your specific preferences and routines. The Echo Show 5 could also become more proactive, anticipating your needs based on past behavior and offering helpful suggestions.

2. New and Improved Visual Features

Future updates may enhance the display, offering more vibrant colors, improved brightness, and better clarity, especially in low-light settings. Amazon could also introduce additional features like customizable screensavers or new widgets that allow for more personalization. You might see features that expand your ability to multitask, such as the ability to view multiple apps or media sources at once.

3. Expanded Smart Home Control

As the Echo Show 5 continues to serve as the hub for controlling smart home devices, expect future updates to improve compatibility with even more devices. Integration with third-party smart devices will likely become smoother, allowing you to control a wider range of products from your Echo Show 5, including thermostats, lights, door locks, and even more specialized appliances. Amazon could also introduce advanced automation features, like the ability to set routines based on time of day, voice commands, or environmental triggers.

4. Audio Enhancements

Updates could further optimize the Echo Show 5's sound performance, improving bass response and audio clarity. With better processing and software improvements, the device may deliver even more powerful sound, making it a better choice for media streaming, video calls, and music. As software evolves, Amazon may also add features like adaptive sound or room calibration, which automatically adjusts the audio based on the acoustics of your space.

5. Advanced Camera Features

The 2-megapixel camera on the Echo Show 5 could receive updates that enhance video quality, especially for video calls. Expect improvements in low-light performance, color accuracy, and real-time video compression. New software features might also offer enhanced security features, such as motion detection or better integration with home security systems.

6. Alexa Skill Expansions

With every software update, you can expect the number of Alexa skills to grow, offering more ways to interact with your Echo Show 5. Amazon could introduce new skills for entertainment, education, productivity, and more, broadening the range of activities that your Echo Show 5 can assist with. New voice commands could make it easier to interact with the device, whether you're managing your day or controlling your smart home.

7. Faster Performance with Software Optimizations

Although the Echo Show 5 is powered by the AZ2 processor, Amazon could continue optimizing the software to make the device even faster. This would result in quicker responses to commands, faster app load times, and a more fluid user experience overall. You might notice that Alexa's voice recognition is quicker, and video streaming or web browsing becomes smoother.

8. Improved Privacy Features

Amazon takes privacy seriously and regularly updates its devices with better security and privacy controls. You can expect future updates to give you even more granular control over your data, such as options to easily manage voice recordings or more transparent privacy settings. Additional features like a physical camera shutter or enhanced data encryption could help you feel even more secure when using the device.

9. New Streaming and Content Partnerships

As the Echo Show 5 continues to be a hub for media consumption, future updates may expand the range of streaming services and apps available for use. Amazon might strike new partnerships with popular video and music platforms to integrate their services directly into the Echo Show 5, allowing you to access content in a more seamless, integrated manner.

10. **Improved** **Multi-Device Functionality:** Amazon may continue to enhance the Echo Show 5's compatibility with other Echo devices, allowing you to create a more cohesive smart home experience. Future updates could allow you to sync audio or video between multiple Echo Show devices or connect with other Amazon devices like Fire TVs or smart speakers, making your home more connected and interactive.

By keeping your Echo Show 5 updated, you'll be able to take advantage of all these improvements, ensuring that your device stays relevant and continues to serve your needs for years to come. Through regular software updates and new features, Amazon will work to make the Echo Show 5 even smarter, more efficient, and more enjoyable to use.

Preparing for Future Innovations

As technology advances at a rapid pace, Echo Show 5 users can expect even more groundbreaking innovations and features that will transform the way we interact with our devices. Amazon's commitment to innovation means that the future of Echo Show 5 is filled with exciting possibilities. Here's how you can prepare for the future of your Echo Show 5, ensuring that you make the most of the innovations to come:

1. Stay Updated with Software Upgrades

Regular software updates are essential to keep your Echo Show 5 functioning at its best. Amazon frequently releases new features, bug fixes, and performance enhancements through software updates. By enabling automatic updates, you ensure that your device always runs the latest version, unlocking new capabilities and improvements as soon as they're available. Keeping your Echo Show 5 updated allows you to enjoy the latest Alexa features, enhanced security, and a smoother experience overall.

2. Prepare for Seamless Smart Home Integration

The smart home landscape is growing rapidly, and Echo Show 5 is central to controlling various devices in your home. With advancements in smart home technology, it's important to stay informed about new smart devices that can integrate with your Echo Show 5. By following updates to Alexa and Amazon's ecosystem, you'll be ready to connect new smart lights, locks, thermostats, cameras, and appliances to your Echo Show 5, making it even more powerful as your home automation hub.

3. Embrace AI and Machine Learning Enhancements

As Amazon continues to advance Alexa's AI and machine learning capabilities, your Echo Show 5 will become even more intuitive and proactive. Future updates may enable Alexa to better anticipate your needs, offer personalized recommendations, and provide more accurate voice recognition. The ability to learn from your interactions will make your Echo Show 5 a more seamless and intelligent assistant, able to carry out more complex tasks without additional input.

4. Exploit Enhanced Multi-Device Capabilities

Amazon is increasingly focused on creating a connected ecosystem across its devices, such as Echo Show, Fire TV, and other smart home products. Preparing for future innovations means thinking about how your Echo Show 5 can interact with other Amazon devices to create a seamless experience. Imagine controlling your smart home with voice commands from any device in your home, or streaming content across multiple Echo devices simultaneously. The future holds exciting possibilities for integrated functionality that will make your devices work together more harmoniously.

5. Get Ready for Upgraded Audio and Visual Features

Audio and video performance is an area that continues to evolve, and future updates may bring improved sound quality, more immersive visuals, and enhanced media streaming features. With each update, your Echo Show 5 could gain new capabilities, such as better display resolution, enhanced color accuracy, or improved sound clarity that adapts to your environment. These upgrades could further solidify the Echo Show 5 as a multimedia hub for everything from video calls to media consumption.

6. Prepare for New Content and Entertainment Features

The entertainment landscape is constantly evolving, with new apps, services, and content available at an ever-growing pace. Echo Show 5's integration with Alexa allows for instant access to music, videos, and more. In the future, Amazon is likely to expand the range of supported streaming services, introduce new entertainment features, and enhance the user interface for seamless navigation. Stay on top of these developments to ensure you're ready to take advantage of new entertainment options as they arrive.

7. Explore Health and Wellness Capabilities

The Echo Show 5 has already begun to integrate health and wellness features like the ability to track fitness and provide reminders for medications or appointments. Looking ahead, Amazon is likely to expand these features, making the Echo Show 5 an even more comprehensive wellness companion. Prepare for innovations that could include health monitoring, stress-relieving activities, and new integrations with fitness apps, all designed to enhance your well-being and promote a healthier lifestyle.

8. Prepare for More Personalized Experiences

As machine learning algorithms improve, your Echo Show 5 will become increasingly adept at providing personalized experiences. From more accurate voice recognition to customized responses based on your preferences, Alexa will become more finely tuned to your individual needs. Preparing for this means taking advantage of customization options, adjusting your settings, and exploring new ways to make your Echo Show 5 uniquely yours.

9. Expect Stronger Privacy and Security Features

Privacy and security are becoming more important than ever, and Amazon is continuously working on improving these aspects across its Echo devices.

Future innovations will likely include more robust privacy controls, allowing you to manage your data more effectively. You may see features like enhanced voice command encryption, stronger camera privacy controls, and increased transparency around data storage. Stay informed about these privacy updates to ensure you're in full control of your data.

10. Anticipate Smarter Integrations with Third-Party Apps

As the Echo Show 5 becomes an even more integral part of the connected home experience, expect new integrations with third-party applications. This will open up exciting possibilities for managing various aspects of your life directly through Alexa. From managing your schedule to interacting with new smart apps, these integrations will enhance your ability to use Echo Show 5 for productivity, entertainment, and home management.

In preparation for these innovations, it's important to continue exploring new features, adjusting your settings as necessary, and remaining engaged with the Echo Show 5 community. By keeping your device updated and learning about the newest advancements, you will be ready to take full advantage of future developments, ensuring that your Echo Show 5 remains a cutting-edge, indispensable part of your everyday life.

Chapter 10:

Troubleshooting and FAQ

While the Echo Show 5 (3rd Gen) is a powerful and reliable device, users may occasionally face some technical difficulties. Below are some of the most common issues you may encounter, along with solutions to troubleshoot and resolve them.

1. Wi-Fi Connectivity Problems

One of the most common issues users face with the Echo Show 5 is difficulty connecting to Wi-Fi or maintaining a stable connection. Here's how to troubleshoot Wi-Fi connectivity problems:

1. **Check Wi-Fi Signal Strength**: Ensure that your Echo Show 5 is within range of a strong Wi-Fi signal. If you're too far from your router, try moving the device closer to improve the connection.

2. **Restart Your Router**: Unplug your router for 30 seconds and then plug it back in. This can help refresh the connection and resolve any temporary issues with the network.

3. **Restart Echo Show 5**: Unplug your Echo Show 5 for about 30 seconds, and plug it back in. This can resolve minor glitches in the connection.

4. **Re-enter Wi-Fi Credentials**: Go to the settings on your Echo Show 5 and manually reconnect to your Wi-Fi network by entering your Wi-Fi password again. This can help if there's an issue with the device's saved credentials.

5. **Check for Interference**: Other electronic devices, thick walls, and large metal objects can interfere with the Wi-Fi signal. Make sure there's nothing blocking the router or the Echo Show 5's connection.

6. **Update Your Wi-Fi Network Settings**: Ensure your router is broadcasting on the 2.4 GHz or 5 GHz bands (depending on what the Echo Show 5 supports) and that it's using the correct encryption type.

7. **Reset Echo Show 5**: If none of the above steps work, try resetting your Echo Show 5 to factory settings and setting it up again.

2. Lagging Performance

If your Echo Show 5 is responding slowly or exhibiting lag in its touchscreen or voice commands, the issue may be related to software, processing power, or connectivity. To resolve this:

1. **Close Unnecessary Apps**: If you have multiple apps or widgets running simultaneously, close them to reduce the load on the device. Too many background apps can slow down performance.

2. **Clear Cache and Data**: If apps like YouTube or Amazon Music are causing lag, try clearing the cache or app data within the device settings. This can help improve the speed of these apps.

3. **Restart the Device**: A restart can often help clear out temporary bugs that cause lag. Unplug the device for 30 seconds, then plug it back in and check the performance.

4. **Software Updates**: Ensure that your Echo Show 5 is up to date with the latest software. Go to the settings and check for available updates, as they often fix bugs or optimize

performance.

5. **Reduce Device Load**: If you have too many connected smart devices using Echo Show 5, try disconnecting or controlling fewer devices at once to ensure it's not overwhelmed.

6. **Reset to Factory Settings**: If lag continues despite following these steps, performing a factory reset may be necessary to restore performance. However, keep in mind this will erase all your settings, so back up important data first.

3. Camera and Video Call Issues

The Echo Show 5 includes a 2-megapixel camera for video calls, but occasionally users may face issues with camera functionality. Here's how to troubleshoot common camera and video call problems:

1. **Check Camera Privacy Settings**: Ensure that the camera is not disabled. Alexa allows you to turn off the camera for privacy reasons. You can enable the camera again through the device's settings or by saying,

"Alexa, turn on the camera."

2. **Clean the Camera Lens**: Dust, smudges, or debris on the camera lens can affect the quality of your video calls. Gently clean the lens with a soft, microfiber cloth to remove any obstructions.

3. **Check for Software Updates**: Sometimes, camera issues are caused by outdated software. Go to the settings menu on your Echo Show 5 to check if there are any updates available for your device.

4. **Check Internet Speed**: Poor internet speed can affect the quality of video calls or even cause the video to freeze. If possible, connect your Echo Show 5 to a stronger Wi-Fi network, or ensure your current network is stable and fast enough for video streaming.

5. **Reboot the Device**: If the camera isn't responding or the video quality is poor, try restarting the Echo Show 5. A simple restart can fix minor glitches affecting the camera.

6. **Test the Camera with a Different App**:
   If you're using the camera for a specific video
   call service like Skype or Zoom, test the
   camera with a different app like Amazon
   Alexa or Amazon Chime to check if the issue
   is app-specific.

7. **Reset Echo Show 5**: As a last resort, if the
   camera continues to malfunction, you may
   need to perform a factory reset. This should
   fix deeper software issues that may be
   affecting the camera's functionality.

By following these troubleshooting steps, you
should be able to address and resolve the most
common issues that may arise with your Echo Show
5. If problems persist, consider reaching out to
Amazon customer support for further assistance.

CONCLUSION

The Echo Show 5 (3rd Gen) is more than just a smart device; it's a transformative addition to your home that can streamline your daily tasks, entertain, and enhance your productivity. Its sleek design, improved performance, and cutting-edge features make it stand out from its predecessors, offering users a truly upgraded experience. From the crystal-clear display to the enhanced audio quality and intuitive voice commands, this smart display provides everything you need to stay connected, entertained, and organized.

As you continue to explore your Echo Show 5, remember that there is so much more beneath the surface. You can take full advantage of its customizable settings, dive deeper into Alexa's capabilities, and maximize its potential for smart home control, media streaming, and productivity tools. It's not just about knowing the basics; it's about discovering hidden features and unlocking the full potential of this remarkable device.

Now that you've gained a comprehensive understanding of how to set up and optimize your Echo Show 5, the journey doesn't end here. Keep experimenting with the various features, exploring new apps, and discovering the endless possibilities that the Echo Show 5 has to offer. With each new update, new features will be introduced, so stay tuned for ways to enhance your experience even further.

Embrace the Echo Show 5 as your new home companion and let it make your daily routines smarter, simpler, and more enjoyable. The more you use it, the more you'll realize just how much this device can do to enhance your life. Welcome to a future where convenience and technology work seamlessly together.